AF429914

INSTANT POT THAI RECIPES COOKBOOK

Everyday Thai Recipes for Beginners

© 2021 All rights reserved

Table of Content

INTRODUCTION

Making Thai Instant Pot is so fast and easy! Also learn my tips to make store-bought red Thai paste taste amazing so that you have meals that's spicy, aromatic and intense.

The beauty of an Instant Pot is how fast and easy it is to cook food in it. Pressure cooking also infuses food with flavour because of how the food is cooked in it. Plus you'll be rewarded with perfectly tender, juicy pieces of chicken.

INSTANT POT CHICKEN PAD THAI

Lately, I'm really into making at-home versions of our favourite takeout dishes. We're eating out a lot less these days, but sometimes we miss a particular meal. This Instant Pot Chicken Pad Thai has quickly become a go-to recipe.

This version of pad Thai is definitely not authentic (well, of course, it's made in a pressure cooker!), but I love that it uses easy-to-find ingredients. Traditional pad Thai sauce includes tamarind paste, but it's not easily found in my local grocery store and I bet not everyone has it on hand. I don't think you'll miss it, once you taste the sauce in this recipe!

Prep Time: 15 mins

Cook Time: 7 mins

Total Time: 37 mins

Servings: 4

Calories: 535 kcal

Ingredients

- 2 tbsp olive oil
- 2 chicken breasts, diced
- 4 cloves garlic minced
- 3 tbsp low-sodium soy sauce or tamari
- 1/2 cup jarred pad thai sauce (I like Thai Kitchen brand)
- 1 1/2 cups water

- 7 oz rice noodles
- 1 cup Carrot matchsticks
- 1/2 each red and yellow pepper, sliced
- 4 green onions, sliced
- 1/3 cup chopped peanuts
- 1/3 cup fresh chopped cilantro

Instructions

1.   Add olive oil, chicken, garlic, soy sauce, pad thai sauce, water and rice noodles to Instant Pot in that order, leaving noodles floating slightly above other ingredients. Set to manual and pressure cook on high for 2 minutes. Instant Pot will take about 10 minutes to pre-heat and then 2 minutes to cook. When complete, press cancel and do a quick release of the steam, waiting until the pressure gauge drops back down and the lid is safe to open.

2.   Add carrot matchsticks, bell peppers and half of peanuts, tossing carefully with tongs. Place lid back on and let sit for 5 minutes.

3.   Remove lid and serve, then top with green onions, remaining chopped peanuts and cilantro. Enjoy!

INSTANT POT CHICKEN FRIED RICE

Instant Pot Chicken Fried Rice is a fast and easy one-pot meal. With simple ingredients like rice, chicken, egg, carrots and peas, your family will love this savory recipe! Perfect for a weeknight dinner or meal prep lunch!

Instant Pot Chicken Fried Rice is quickly becoming a go-to recipe for my lunch meal prep. It's incredibly easy to throw together and even my 5-year-old likes it as a hot school lunch. I know what you're thinking – this rice isn't actually fried. I know, I know. But this recipe is a great option if you don't have leftover cooked rice!

Instant Pot Chicken Fried Rice is awesome because:

- it requires just 10 ingredients (plus garnishes)
- it's made in one pot – even the egg is scrambled in the Instant Pot!
- there's minimal prep work
- you only need about 30 minutes to make it

No need for takeout when you have this recipe!

Prep time: 10 mins

Cook Time: 6 mins

Total Time: 36 mins

Servings: 4

Calories: 489 kcal

Ingredients:

Here's what you'll need to make it. See the recipe card below for exact quantities and detailed instructions!

- **Vegetable oil** – for sautéing
- **Eggs**
- **Garlic**
- **Chicken broth** – 1 1/4 cups; normally you would use a 1:1 ratio rice to liquid, but the chicken and carrots release liquid during cooking and add to the broth. I tested with 1 1/2 cups broth and found the dish had too much moisture for a "fried" rice.
- **Chicken breast**
- **Carrots**
- **Jasmine rice** – rinsed really well until the water is clear. You want to remove as much starch as possible so the texture of the rice won't be too sticky.
- **Frozen green peas** – I run them under warm water and drain thoroughly before stirring them into the cooked rice.
- **Soy sauce** – or wheat-free tamari, if gluten free. Use a low-sodium variety and adjust the amount to suit your taste.
- **Sesame oil** – to add nice flavour
- **Green onion & hot sauce** – for garnish, optional

Instructions:

1.   Scramble the egg. Turn on the Sauté function on the Instant Pot and heat 1 teaspoon of vegetable oil. Add the whisked egg and use a spatula to push it around until it's scrambled and cooked through. Transfer the egg to a plate and set aside. There may be some egg stuck to the bottom of the insert – that's okay at this step.

2:      Here another teaspoon of vegetable oil, then add

the minced garlic. Sauté the garlic for about a minute, until fragrant. Turn off the Sauté function, then pour in a small amount of chicken broth and use a spatula to deglaze the insert. Scrape up every bit of food that is stuck to the bottom. This will prevent a burn warning.

3.   Add the remaining broth, then evenly layer the diced chicken breast, diced carrots and rice (*in this order*). Push the rice into the broth so it's submerged, but *do not stir.*

4.   Place the lid on the Instant Pot and set the vent to sealing. Cook on Manual High pressure for 3 minutes with the keep warming setting turned off. At the end of cooking time, allow the pressure to release naturally

for 10 minutes, then quick release any remaining pressure.

5. Mix in the soy sauce and sesame oil until the rice is evenly coated, then stir in the peas and reserved scrambled egg. Set the lid askew on the pot for a minute or two to let the peas and egg warm up. Serve immediately with your chosen garnishes or divide into meal prep containers. Be sure to let the rice cool completely before refrigerating. Eat within 4 days.

Tips for success

1. Rinse the rice very well. This will remove excess starch and reduce the stickiness of the cooked dish.

2. Use a long-grain white rice. My preference is jasmine rice, but generic long-grain white should work, too. Note that I find generic white rice can turn out more "mushy" than jasmine. I suspect it's a quality thing. Brown rice requires a much longer cooking time, so will not work with this recipe. If you use basmati, I would add a minute of cook time as I find it stays more al dente than jasmine.

3. Deglaze the insert. Do not skip this step! If there's any food stuck to the bottom of the insert, you may get a burn warning.

4. Submerge the rice in the broth. Be sure all the rice is pushed into the broth. This will help it cook evenly.

INSTANT POT CHICKEN AND RICE SOUP

Chicken and rice soup is one of those meals that I crave when the temperatures drop or when one of the season's pesky colds or coughs takes hold. No matter how much hand washing and Vitamin C popping we do, at least one virus manages to sweep through the family each year. Homemade soup recipes are the best tonic as soon as the sneezing and sniffling starts.

Out comes the Instant Pot for some chicken rice soup love! And why do I like making this soup in the Instant Pot as opposed to using the stovetop?

Prep Time: 5 minutes

Cook Time: 17 minutes

Total Time: 37 minutes

Servings: 7

Calories: 240.8kcal

Ingredients

- 2 teaspoons olive oil
- ½ yellow onion chopped
- 1 large carrot cut into thin half-circles
- 1 large stalk celery diced
- 3 garlic cloves minced
- 1 teaspoon dried thyme
- ¾ teaspoon crushed dried rosemary
- 5 cups low sodium chicken broth
- 1 pounds boneless skinless chicken breasts
- ¾ cup brown rice uncooked
- 1/2 teaspoon salt

- ¼ teaspoon ground pepper
- ¼ cup minced flat-leaf parsley
- salt & pepper to taste

Instructions

1.   Set the Instant Pot to Saute mode. Heat the olive oil, then add the onion, carrot and celery. Saute the vegetables, stirring occasionally, until starting to soften, 3 to 4 minutes.

2.   Add the garlic, thyme and rosemary. Cook, stirring constantly, for 30 seconds.

3.   Pour in the chicken broth and stir to combine.

4.   Add the chicken breasts, brown rice, salt and pepper to the Instant Pot.

5.   Put the lid on the Instant Pot, close the steam vent and set to HIGH pressure using the manual setting. Set the time to 13 minutes. It will take the Instant Pot about 15 minutes to reach pressure.

6.   Once the time is expired, use natural release for 10 minutes, then quick release.

7.   Transfer the chicken breasts to a cutting board, shred with 2 forks, then transfer back to the Instant Pot. Stir in the parsley and season with salt and pepper to taste. Serve.

INSTANT POT THAI CHICKEN CURRY

Packed with amazing flavour and simple, wholesome ingredients, this Instant Pot Thai Chicken Curry will become a regular on your dinner rotation. Made with chicken breasts, coconut milk, green curry paste and tender-crisp vegetables like carrots and bell pepper, your family will love this easy meal.

Prep Time: 15 minutes

Cook Time: 15 minutes

Total Time: 30 minutes

Servings: 6 servings

Calories: 246 kcal

Ingredients:

- 2 teaspoons coconut oil
- 1 yellow onion, small dice
- 1 tablespoon grated fresh ginger or ginger paste
- 1/4 cup chicken broth or water
- 1 14 oz can coconut milk
- 3 tablespoons Thai green curry paste
- 1 tablespoon wheat-free tamari (or soy sauce if not gluten free, or coconut aminos to avoid soy)
- 1 lb boneless skinless chicken breast (see note 3)
- 1 red bell pepper, thinly sliced and then again in half
- 2 carrots, cut into large matchsticks
- 1 handful spinach, roughly chopped
- 1-2 teaspoons brown sugar (or coconut sugar)
- Freshly squeezed lime juice (to taste)

Instructions:

1.   Turn on the sauté function on your Instant Pot and heat the coconut oil. Sauté the diced onion until softening and fragrant, about 3 minutes. Add the ginger paste and continue to sauté another 30 seconds. Turn off the sauté function.

2.   Pour in the broth or water and deglaze the insert (use a spatula to scrape up any food that's stuck to the bottom). Then, add the coconut milk, curry paste, and tamari and whisk until smooth.

3.   Place the chicken breasts in the coconut milk mixture. Put the top on the Instant Pot, set the vent to sealing and cook on Manual High Pressure for 10 minutes (see note 3 for how to adjust cook time for diced chicken breast). At the end of cooking time, allow for 10 minutes natural pressure release, then quick release any remaining pressure.

4.   Remove the chicken breasts to a large plate and pull it apart into pieces (not quite a full shred). Meanwhile, turn on the Sauté function on the Instant Pot and add the bell pepper, carrots, spinach and brown sugar. Simmer for 3 to 5 minutes, or until the vegetables reach your desired texture.

5.   Once you're done shredding the chicken, add it back to the Instant Pot to warm up and squeeze in a

bit of lime juice, to taste. Turn off the Sauté function and serve immediately with your favourite rice and fresh cilantro. Store any leftovers in the refrigerator in a sealed container and eat within 4 days.

Notes:

1. This recipe was tested in a 6-quart Instant Pot model.
2. Inactive time indicates the time needed for the Instant Pot to come to pressure and release pressure.
3. If you prefer the texture of diced chicken over shredded chicken, cut the chicken breast into bite-sized pieces and adjust the cook time down to 4 minutes. Do a natural pressure release for 5-10 minutes before releasing the remaining pressure.
4. Nutrition estimate is for the curry only (without rice), using full-fat coconut milk.

INSTANT POT CHICKEN NOODLE SOUP

This recipe has all the ingredients you'd expect to find in a classic chicken noodle soup, plus a few additions that really should belong in every recipe, like garlic, ginger, turmeric, and a bit of cayenne too.

Everyone who has tried this chicken soup really likes it – my young kids, my (picky) husband, our friends, and neighbors. For this reason, I feel pretty good about stating that this might just be one of the best chicken noodle soup recipes out there.

Prep Time: 10 minutes

Cook Time: 10 minutes

Total Time: 20 minutes

Servings: 6 servings

Calories: 198

Ingredients:

- 2 tablespoons butter
- 1 onion diced (approx 2 to 3 cups diced)
- 1 ½ cups celery slices 3 sticks of celery

- 4 teaspoons minced garlic
- 2 teaspoons minced ginger
- 2 pounds boneless skinless chicken thighs, quartered
- 2 tablespoons fresh thyme leaves
- 2 teaspoons salt to taste
- 1 teaspoon freshly ground black pepper to taste
- 1 teaspoon dried oregano
- ½ teaspoon turmeric
- ¼ teaspoon cayenne to taste
- 8 cups chicken broth

Add Later:

- 2 cups carrots coins approx 4 carrots peeled and chopped
- 8 ounces wide egg noodles or noodles of your choice gluten-free works too
- 3 tablespoons finely chopped fresh flat-leaf parsley leaves plus extra for garnish.

Instructions:

1. Press sauté and adjust heat to the highest setting. Add butter and once it melts, add the onion, celery, garlic, ginger, and sauté for 5 minutes, or until onion softens and becomes translucent.

2.   Add the remaining ingredients to the pot and mix well.

3.   Secure the lid, close the pressure valve, and cook for 5 minutes at high pressure.

4.   Quick-release pressure.

5.   Press the sauté button (the heat should still be on the highest setting - if not, adjust it), and add the carrots.

6.   Now wait for the pot to come to a full boil (this takes about 8 minutes), then add the noodles to the pot and mix well. Cook for 5 to 7 minutes uncovered, or until the noodles are tender.

7.   Add parsley, stir, taste for seasoning, and adjust if necessary.

8.   Pour into a bowl and garnish with additional parsley leaves and serve.

Notes

- Egg noodles absorb broth as they sit, you may need to add more broth when reheating leftovers.
- If using a different type of noodle, follow the cook time listed on the package.

INSTANT POT THAI PEANUT NOODLES

Instant Pot Thai Peanut Noodles – easy one-pot vegetarian weeknight meal which gets done in less than 30 minutes!

One of the cuisines that I actually liked after moving to US was Thai. My exposure to different kind of food/cuisine in India was limited. I hardly ever ate anything other than Indian. We grew up eating homemade food everyday and it was always Indian – the same dal, rice, sabzi (veggie) and roti. That's pretty much all I ate for lunch and dinner. When I moved to US, I was exposed to an array of flavors. These flavors were so different and I had never tasted them before. I tried a lot of new food, some which I didn't like at all and some I loved like Thai food!

Do you guys love thai food? I think its so flavorful and its hard not to like it. While I love eating it out, I often make it at home too. These Instant Pot Thai Peanut Noddles are so easy to make in the IP. It's a one pot meal which you can put on the table in less than 30 minutes!

What makes these Instant Pot Thai Peanut Noodles special?

- ✓ these get done in one pot – no need to cook the noodles separately.
- ✓ one pot means less dirty dishes!
- ✓ gets done in less than 30 minutes!
- ✓ perfect meal for those busy nights.
- ✓ packed with flavors, there's soy sauce, honey, peanut butter, sriracha and rice vinegar in there.
- ✓ make it vegan be replacing the honey with brown sugar or any other vegan friendly sweetener.

To make these instant pot thai peanut noodles, all you need is to chop the ginger, garlic, pepper, carrot and green onion. Once you have these chopped, it only takes 5 minutes to put it all in the pot and then let the IP do its thing. *You may also add tofu to these noodles to make the meal protein-rich.* Sarvesh is not very fond of tofu and hence I skipped that part.

We add uncooked spaghetti to the Instant Pot along with the veggies and sauce and it all gets perfectly cooked. Isn't that amazing? Seriously I can't get over the fact that I don't have to boil the noodles separately. And they get perfectly cooked, not soggy at all. In fact the spaghetti was al-dente which means that it had a nice bite to it. If you prefer softer noodles, then you may increase the cooking time by couple of minutes. This was perfect for me.

The garnishes add more flavor to these thai peanut noodles. So don't forget to add in lots of chopped cilantro, lime juice and crushed peanuts! If you have never made noodles/spaghetti in your Instant Pot, now is the time! And this is the easiest recipe to start with. I am sure once you make it, you will be amazed how easy it really was. Hope you guys enjoy this one!

Thai Peanut Noodles made in the Instant Pot! Easy one-pot weeknight meal which gets done in less than 30 minutes!

Prep Time: 10 mins

Cook Time: 15 mins

Total Time: 25 mins

Servings: 2

Calories: 678 kcal

Ingredients:

- 2 tablespoons oil I used vegetable oil
- 4-5 garlic cloves minced
- 1 inch ginger minced
- 2 medium carrots 100 grams, sliced thin
- 1 medium red pepper 200 grams, sliced thin
- 3 stalks green onion finely chopped
- 2.5 tablespoons soy sauce
- 1.5 tablespoons rice vinegar
- 1.5 tablespoons honey or to taste
- 1 tablespoon sriracha or to taste
- 3 tabelspoons peanut butter
- salt to taste
- 8 oz spaghetti broken into half
- 1.5 cups water 12 oz
- 2 tablespoons chopped cilantro
- juice of 1 lime
- crushed peanuts to garnish

Intructions:

1. Press the saute button on your Instant Pot. Once

it displays hot, add oil and then add the minced garlic and ginger. Saute for a minute until garlic and ginger start changing color.

2.   Add in the veggies - carrots, pepper and green onion and toss to combine. You may reserve some spring onion greens for garnish.

3.   Push veggies to the side and to the center of the pot add the soy sauce, rice vinegar, honey, sriracha, peanut butter and salt.

4.   Whisk to combine the sauce. You may also combine the sauce beforehand in a bowl.

5.   Break spaghetti into half and then add to the pot. Add water until spaghetti is just covered. You may press the noodles slightly with a spatula so that noodles on top get slightly under water.

6.   Close the pot with its lid. Press the manual or pressure cook button and cook on high pressure for 4 minutes. The pressure valve should be in the sealing position. Do a quick pressure release.

7.   Open the pot, use a tong to mix the sauce, noodles and veggies together.

8.   Add reserved green onion greens, juice of 1 lime and cilantro. Serve the noodles with crushed peanuts on top!

Notes:

1. The noodles will look little watery when you open the pot but soak the sauce pretty quickly.
2. The noodles are Al dente at 4 minutes. Cook for couple more minutes for softer noodles
3. Adjust sriracha and honey to taste. If you like spicy noodles, add more of sriracha.

INSTANT POT THAI PEANUT TOFU PINEAPPLE CURRY

The next recipe in the Instant Pot series – Thai Peanut Tofu Pineapple Curry. The recipe is vegan and all made in the instant pot!

The concept of pressure cooker is deep rooted in Indian culture and cooking. We have been cooking our lentils, beans, rice in the pressure cooker since eternity. Have I told you guys my pressure cooker story? So this is one kitchen gadget which every Indian carries along when they leave India. Yes, we are almost handicapped without a pressure cooker in the kitchen.

So what happened was when I was going to Scotland for masters, my mom packed my tiny pressure cooker in my carry on luggage. I didn't even check my bag and mom thought such an important thing cannot be placed in the check in baggage! (of course!!) Well the cooker ended up being taken out at the airport security. I remember requesting them to let me take it since I was a student and going to a new country but they didn't budge.

I was so disappointed and then couldn't cook anything there because a) I hardly knew any cooking!

and b) without pressure cooker, whatever I knew was also a challenge. Mom dad ultimately couriered the cooker to me! Well now you understand the importance of a pressure cooker for an Indian!

Moving on to this curry, the inspiration for this dish comes from a dish that I ate at a local Thai restaurant. The curry had cashews and pineapple and I really liked it. So I thought of adding some tofu, peanut butter and making it more wholesome! Here's the thing with peanut butter in curries, it can get really overwhelming.

For this recipe, I would suggest starting with 2 tablespoons of peanut butter. If you like a stronger flavor, you may add 2 tablespoons more. But don't start with 4 tablespoons in the first place. This thai peanut tofu pineapple curry is a sweet and spicy curry. You may adjust the flavors to taste. Prefer a spicier curry? Add more of the dried red chili, thai red curry paste and sriracha. Like a sweeter curry? Add more pineapple and coconut sugar!

This instant pot recipe is vegan and can be made gluten-free by using tamari (gluten-free substitute for soy sauce). Now before someone says that the thai red curry paste has fish sauce so how come it's vegan,? Well I use "Thai Kitchen" red curry paste and it's completely vegan and easily available at most grocery stores and also on amazon.

Prep Time: 10 mins

Cook Time: 15 mins

Total Time: 25 mins

Servings: 3

Calories: 354 kcal

Ingredients:

- 1 tablespoon olive oil
- 2 dried red chili broken into pieces
- 1 small white onion chopped
- 1/4 cup raw cashews
- 2 teaspoon grated garlic
- 2 teaspoons grated ginger
- 2-3 tablespoons peanut butter or more for a stronger peanut flavor
- 14 oz can coconut milk I use light you may use full fat
- 2 tablespoons + 1 teaspoon thai red curry paste
- 1/2 cup water
- 1 teaspoon soy sauce or tamari if gluten-free
- 3 teaspoon rice vinegar
- 1.5 teaspoon sriracha adjust to taste
- 1-2 teaspoon coconut sugar adjust to taste
- 1/4 teaspoon turmeric powder
- salt to taste
- 200 grams extra-firm tofu cut into cubes
- 1/3 cup pineapple cubes I used canned pineapple cubes
- juice of 1 lime

- cilantro to garnish

Instructions:

1.   Press saute mode on instant pot, once the pot heats up add olive oil. Break the dried red chili into two and add to the oil.
2.   Add onion and saute for a minute. Add cashews and saute till they start changing color.
3.   Add grated ginger and garlic and saute for a minute till you get nice aroma.
4.   Meanwhile in a bowl whisk together peanut butter, coconut milk, water and thai red curry paste. You might need to heat this mixture a little so that the peanut butter mixes completely.
5.   Add this mixture to the pot once ginger-garlic are fragrant. Give it a good stir.
6.   Then add soy sauce, rice vinegar, sriracha, coconut sugar, turmeric powder and salt. Stir to combine.
7.   Now add cubed tofu pieces to the pot and mix. I used extra-firm tofu and pressed it with a hard object for 20 minutes prior to using it in the recipe.
8.   Cover the lid, cancel the saute mode. Press the manual button, adjust pressure to high and and cook on manual high pressure for 2 minutes.

9.   Quick release as soon as 2 minutes are up.

10.   Cancel "keep warm" mode and press the saute mode again.

11.   Add pineapple pieces and let it simmer for 1-2 minutes. You can adjust consistency of the curry at this point. Add water if it's too thick for your liking.

12.   Squeeze in some fresh lime juice.

13.   Garnish with cilantro and serve the thai peanut tofu pineapple curry with rice!

INSTANT POT THAI COCONUT SOUP

Instant Pot Thai Coconut Soup is a delicious, comforting vegetarian Thai recipe which takes less than 10 minutes to cook! Includes tofu or chicken options!

Whenever we go to a Thai restaurant, I have to order the Coconut Soup; It's magically delicious!!! So creamy, yet slightly spicy and sweet, it's amazingly tasty and I crave it all the time. For a long time I thought the authentic Thai flavors were difficult to recreate at home, but I was wrong, it's actually very easy when you have the right ingredients. This Instant Pot Thai Coconut soup only takes 4 minutes to cook in the instant pot (plus the time to come to pressure etc), and turns out fantastic. I like using tofu in my coconut soup, but a lot of people enjoy the soup with chicken, so I will include those instructions below as well. You are going to LOVE this comforting Instant Pot Thai Coconut Soup!

Prep Time: 5 mins

Cook Time: 10 mins

Total Time: 15 mins

Servings: 6 servings

Calories: 202 kcal

Ingredients:

- 1 TBS sesame oil
- 1 medium white onion, sliced
- 1 medium red bell pepper, seeded and sliced

- 8 ounces mushrooms, wiped clean, cut in halves or 4ths if larger
- 1 TBS brown sugar
- 1 TBS fresh ginger, about an inch diced
- 2 TBS Thai red curry paste
- 1 1/2 TBS fish sauce
- 1 TBS reduced sodium soy sauce
- 1 block firm or extra firm tofu, drained and cut into bite sized peices
- 4 cups vegetable or chicken broth
- 3 TBS lime juice
- 1 cup unsweetened coconut milk, (found in the Asian area of the grocery store, usually in a can)
- sriracha to taste , I typically add 1 tsp
- lime wedges for garnish
- cilantro for garnish

Instructions:

1. Heat a 6 or 8 quart Instant Pot, using the sauté function. Add oil, onions, and peppers and sauté 2-3 minutes. **If you are going to add chicken, this is when you should do it (see notes below).

2. Add the mushrooms, and cook for 2 minutes. Add brown sugar, ginger, curry paste,

fish sauce, lite soy sauce and stir. Add tofu then broth.

3. Close the lid, seal the pressure valve, and set on manual/high for 4 minutes.

4. Once the time is up, let the pressure release naturally for 5-10 minutes, then flip the valve to release the remaining pressure (careful some liquid may spout out). Remove the top carefully.

5. Add lime juice, coconut milk, and sriracha to taste. Stir everything to combine.

6. Serve the soup and garnish with lime wedges and cilantro. Enjoy!

Recipe Notes:

TIP: You should remember when using the Instant Pot, that the time it takes to cook the recipe (4 mins), is not the total time of the recipe. You need to give the pot some time to 'come to pressure'. With a soup this will take a bit of time since there is a lot of liquid, probably 10-15 minutes. Once it comes to pressure the pot will beep and the time will begin counting down.

If using CHICKEN:

- 1lb boneless skinless chicken breast, sliced into 1/2 inch strips or bit sized cubes.

- Add the chicken at the end of step one, with the peppers and onions, and cook. Continue with recipe as written. *Omit tofu.*

Nutrition info for TOFU: 202 calories, 12g fat, 7g saturated fat, 14g carbohydrates, 2g fiber, 7g sugar, 9g protein.

Nutrition info for CHICKEN (no tofu): 215 calories, 10g fat, 6g saturated fat, 13g carbohydrates, 2g fiber, 7g sugar, 17g protein.

INSTANT POT CHICKEN LETTUCE WRAPS

One of our favorite copycat recipes of restaurant meals are lettuce wraps. They are so easy and so fun to make and eat! You can fill lettuce wraps with so many different fillings. My go-to is ground chicken cooked in hoisin sauce, soy sauce, vinegar, garlic, sweet chili sauce and ginger, whisked together into one flavor-packed mixture. It is flavorful and delicious!

Instant Pot Chicken Lettuce Wraps Recipe - quick and easy lettuce wraps filled with ground chicken cooked in Asian sauce. Perfect dinner idea for busy weeknights!

Prep Time: 2 mins

Cook Time: 15 mins

Total Time: 17 mins

Servings: 4 servings

Calories: 334 kcal

Ingredients

- 1 tablespoon vegetable oil
- 2 teaspoon sesame oil
- 1 lb ground chicken
- 1/2 teaspoon salt
- 1/4 teaspoon black pepper
- 1 small yellow onion chopped
- 2 cloves garlic minced
- 1/4 cup chicken stock
- 1/4 cup hoisin sauce
- 3 tablespoons low-sodium soy sauce
- 1 tablespoon apple cider vinegar or rice vinegar
- 1 teaspoon sesame oil
- 2 tablespoons sweet chili sauce
- 1 teaspoon ground ginger
- 8 oz. can water chestnuts drained

- 8 leaves of butter lettuce

Instructions

1. Make sure the stainless steel insert is in your Instant Pot. Press "saute" setting and wait 1 minute. Add vegetable and sesame oil to insert and let heat up.
2. Add ground chicken to Instant Pot and cook, breaking down with wooden spoon. Season with salt and pepper. Add onion and garlic. Cook until chicken is no longer pink. Press "cancel/off" button.
3. Add 1/4 cup of chicken broth and deglaze the bottom of the pot.
4. In a small mixing bowl or measuring cup, whisk together hoisin sauce, soy sauce, sesame oil, vinegar, ginger and sweet chili sauce. Pour mixture over chicken and stir well.
5. Close the lid, set valve to sealing position (newer models do it on their own). Make sure the IP is set to cook at HIGH pressure. Press "manual" setting and set timer to 4 minutes.
6. When the timer is done, let the pressure release naturally for at least 10 minutes.
7. Carefully open the lid away from your face. Stir

chicken.

8. Add chopped water chestnuts to chicken and stir.
9. Place up to 1/4 cup of mixture onto each lettuce leaf. Serve immediately.

Recipe Notes

If you don't have ground chicken on hand, you can slice boneless skinless chicken breast into slices, partially freeze it (20 to 30 minutes in the freezer should do it), then pulse in the food processor until you reach desired texture. If you don't like or have chicken on hand, you can also make this recipe with ground turkey.

INSTANT POT THAI GREEN CURRY WITH CHICKEN

Instant Pot Thai Green Curry is a creamy coconut curry with the flavors of green chilies, Thai Basil, lime, coriander, and cumin. This spicy curry is as good as your favorite restaurant Thai green curry but is so quick and easy that it can be ready in less than 30 minutes. Serve it with Instant Pot Jasmine Rice for an amazing flavor combination!

Prep Time: 15 minutes

Cook Time: 15 minutes

Total Time: 30 minutes

Servings: 6

Calories: 211 kcal

Ingredients

- 3 Tbsp Thai Green curry paste – preferably Maesri or Mae Ploy brand
- 14 oz. coconut milk – (1 can), preferably Aroy D or Chaokoh brand
- 1 tsp coriander powder
- 1/2 tsp cumin powder
- 1 lb boneless skinless chicken thighs – sliced into thin bite-size pieces
- 1/4 cup chicken broth – or water
- 2 Tbsp fish sauce – more to taste
- 1 Tbsp brown sugar – or to taste
- 1 Tbsp lime juice
- 1 cup green bell pepper – cubed or strips
- 1 cup zucchini – sliced or strips
- 1/2 cup onion – cubed
- 1/2 cup bamboo shoots – canned, sliced
- 4 lime leaves – slightly bruised
- 1/4 cup Thai Basil leaves

Instructions:

1.   Select *Saute* mode and stir in green curry paste and 1/2 can of coconut milk until mixture is bubbly, about a minute or two.

2.   Stir in coriander and cumin and cook for 30 seconds.

3.   Press *Cancel*.

4.   Stir in chicken, remaining coconut milk, and chicken broth.

5.   Close Instant Pot and pressure cook on *High Pressure* for 4 minutes.

6.   Do a Quick Release of pressure (QR) and open the Instant Pot.

7.   Add in fish sauce, brown sugar, lime juice, bell pepper, zucchini, onions, bamboo shoots, and lime leaves.

8.   Select *Saute* and cook until vegetables are crisp-tender, 3 to 5 minutes. (Be sure not to overcook. Vegetables will continue to cook in the residual heat.)

9.   Taste and adjust with more fish sauce, brown sugar or lime juice.

10.   Stir in the Thai basil leaves.

11.   Serve with Instant Pot Jasmine Rice.